204 G
Guiteau, Charles J.
The truth
30049003236453

Piqua Public Library
116 West High Street
Piqua, Ohio 45356

Discarded

The Truth

A Companion to the Bible

by
Charles J. Guiteau

Silver Street Media
Agawam, Massachusetts

ISBN 978-1-59838-026-2
Republished in 2011

Reprinted by Silver Street Media
from original edition published by
Donnelley, Gassette and Loyd
in 1879.

www.silverstreetmedia.com

A BOOK FOR EVERY ONE TO READ.

THE TRUTH:

A

COMPANION TO THE BIBLE.

BY CHARLES J. GUITEAU,
Lawyer, Theologian and Lecturer.

CHICAGO:
DONNELLEY, GASSETTE & LOYD.
1879.

COPYRIGHTED 1879,
DONNELLEY, GASSETTE & LOYD,
CHICAGO.

PREFACE.

A new line of thought runs through this book, and the Author asks for it a careful attention, to the end, that many souls may find the Savior.

A REPLY

TO

RECENT ATTACKS ON THE BIBLE.

Attacks on the Bible.

CHRISTENDOM holds that the Bible is God's word; that it was written by holy men, and that its spirit and character emanated from God.

WHY SOME PEOPLE ARE INFIDELS.

Any rational mind can find abundant evidence in the Bible to sustain Christianity, and the fact that some people denounce Christianity is conclusive evidence that they have not examined the Bible with steady, persevering gaze. "The cares of this world, and the deceitfulness of riches, and the lusts of other things" have paralyzed their thought, and so they fall into infidelity. "My sheep," says Christ, "hear my voice," and the Bible is Christ's voice speaking to the world.

WHAT NEW YORK MINISTERS SAY ABOUT HELL.

Dr. John Hall, of New York, preached recently on hell, and among other things said, "Those ministers who attacked the orthodox doctrine of eternal punishment were generally uneducated men." By this Dr. Hall meant they were not scholars. Dr. Farrar was of this class. He was not disciplined in the accuracy of logical thinking. He was eloquent, but not correct. "Gehenna meant hell, eternal hell," said Dr. Hall, "and nothing short of it, as every scholar knew."

Dr. Fulton, of Brooklyn, agrees with Dr. Hall, and adds, "Hell is the prison-house of the damned."

"It is a minister's duty," says Dr. Fulton, "when he sees an unbeliever in his congregation, to preach to him: —You will go to hell if you don't believe in Jesus Christ." No matter what Darwin, Huxley, or any one else says:— "The question is whether they agree with the Bible."

AN INFIDEL'S VIEWS.

"Hell is for tramps, not for the rich," says a noted infidel; but listen to the apostle James:—

"Go to, now, ye rich, weep and howl, for your miseries that shall come upon you. Your riches are corrupted, and your garments are moth-eaten. Your gold and silver are cankered, and shall be a witness against you. It shall eat your flesh as with *fire*. For ye have lived in pleasure on the earth, and been wanton."

THE SOUL IMMORTAL.

A noted infidel denies the immortality of the soul.

"I am willing to give up heaven," he says, "to get rid of hell."

We prove the immortality of the soul thus: We read "that the Lord God formed man of the dust of the ground and breathed into his nostrils the breath of life, and man became a living soul." (Gen. ii: 7.) Man, therefore, was composed of two substances, the dust of the ground and the breath of life, *i. e.* matter and spirit.

We hold that "a spirit is a fluid. That it has many of the properties of caloric, electricity, galvanism, and magnetism. That it also has the power of assimilation, growth, and self-originating motion. That it has personality, feeling, intelligence and will." When Adam was created, the Almighty breathed this vital fluid into Adam's body and he then became a living soul. As soon as this vital fluid (or the Almighty's breath) entered into Adam's dust-formed body, it partook of the shape of that body, *i. e.* it became congealed, and ever afterwards retained the form and shape of that body.

The prime element of the soul is this vital fluid which emanated from the Almighty, and it is *this* eternal spirit which makes the soul indestructible. "He that believeth on me," says Christ, "shall never die." Why? Because the life of the soul and body are *one*. The soul lives after it has left the body. Every human being is destined for heaven or hell; because they have a soul, and *that* is immortal.

THE BIBLE.

The Bible is the record of God's dealings with man. By it He spoke to the Jewish nation. By it Christ and the apostles thunder their proclamations across the ages since the destruction of Jerusalem, and on it we base our hope of eternal life. For five years, at home and abroad, our friend Moody has told us of "the love of God in Jesus Christ," as revealed in the Bible. For centuries it has stood Satan's fire. For centuries it has been read and wept over by millions of the best men and women who have lived "in this vale of tears," and it will take a great many infidels to destroy the faith of Christendom in the Bible.

"What is the Bible, any way?" shouts a noted infidel, with a brazen air.

"The Old Testament," he says, "is filled with curses, revenge, hate, barbarity, brutality." We admit it is full of murders, wars, rapine. But God is not responsible for *that*.

We now propose to rapidly review the principal narratives contained in the Bible, to the end we may show the character of that book.

"In the beginning," we read, "God created the heavens and the earth and all things that dwell therein, and pronounced it very good;" that He made man "in His own image," and gave him "a wife;" that He put the man and the woman into the Garden of Eden, and gave the man full dominion over all created things. And God commanded the man, saying, of every tree of the garden thou mayest freely eat; but of the tree of the knowledge of good and evil thou shalt not eat, for in the day thou eatest thereof thou shalt surely *die*. We also read that Satan, in the form of a serpent, said unto the woman, "Ye can eat, and ye shall not die;" that thereupon the woman ate the forbidden fruit, and then induced the man to eat.

That, soon thereafter, the "Lord God called unto Adam, and said, Where art thou? Hast thou eaten of the tree whereof I commanded thee, saying, thou shalt not eat? The man said, I did eat," and blamed it on the woman, and the woman blamed it on the serpent: so they both got out of it.

Now what happened?

And the Almighty was angry; he cursed the man, the woman, and the serpent; he pronounced a special curse upon each.

THE ATONEMENT.

And here we must touch briefly upon the atonement, and show how God became reconciled to man through the death and resurrection of Jesus Christ.

When Adam sinned he threw himself into the arms of the devil. His posterity, in consequence of his surrender, came into being under a law of gravitation towards sin and death. We take the orthodox view of human depravity and hold that the "whole world lieth in the wicked one." We also hold, that a part of mankind are not only born under the power of "the wicked one," but are of his seed, and that their destination is perdition.

We also hold that another part of mankind are of Christ's seed and that their destination is heaven. " My sheep," says Christ, " hear my voice." The reason some people must be damned is because they have no ear to hear the gospel of God's reconciliation with man, through the death and resurrection of Jesus Christ.

By the death and resurrection of Christ, God became reconciled to human nature, and what the race lost by Adam's fall they gained by the ascension of Christ. Jesus Christ by his death and resurrection overcame the devil. He released man from his grasp and thereby destroyed the cause of all sin, and thereby reconciled human nature to God. The effect of this action on them that believe is to release them from the power of sin; on them that believe not, to consign them with the devil to eternal damnation. No one will be damned without a chance to believe on Christ. If they reject Christ they must be damned. It is *their* fault; not God's.

"But," says a noted infidel (and this is his great point), "hell being such a terrible, awful place, and God being so *very* good, He won't send any one there." We answer, God must sustain his government. Heaven is for the righteous. Hell for the wicked. Heaven would be a hell, if the wicked could get into it. Hell is for the devil's seed; heaven for Christ's seed.

THE BIBLE GOD'S WORD.

Christendom holds the Bible is God's word, and we further show that it is God's word.

About a thousand years after Adam, we read that God saw that "the wickedness of man was great, and He repented that He had made man," and said, "I will destroy man, whom I have created, from the face of the earth." There was only one righteous man in all the world. His name was Noah. "And God said unto Noah, the end of all flesh is come;" make thee an ark, for I am going "to destroy all flesh." And Noah *did* as the Lord commanded. Now what? After Noah and his family and his property were safely in the ark, "the fountains of the great deep were broken up, and the windows of heaven were opened," and the rain descended in torrents for forty days and forty nights, and every living thing on earth was destroyed—save Noah and his ark.

The point of this story is that God KEPT His word, and He always keeps His word.

What next? A thousand years after Noah came Abraham. "And God said to Abraham, get thee out of thy country, and from thy kindred, and from thy father's house, unto a land that I shall show thee; and I will make of thee a great nation; and I will bless thee, and make thy name great; and thou shalt be a blessing; and I will bless them that bless thee; and curse him that curseth thee; and in thee shall all families of the earth be blessed." (Gen. xii: 1–3.) Now what? "And Abraham did as the Lord had spoken." Abraham's obedience was the foundation of God's favor. The Old Testament is the record of God's dealings with Abraham and his seed for two thousand years—*i. e.* till the birth of Christ.

The New Testament, which is a record of Christ's life and principles, is simply a continuation of God's dealings with mankind. Christ endorsed the Old Testament in every possible way. He always spoke of it with the utmost respect, and said He came not to destroy "the law, but to fulfill it." "Search the scriptures," he says, "for in them ye think ye have eternal life, and they are they which testify of me." "Had ye believed Moses, ye would have believed me, for he wrote of me."

Infidels say the Old Testament is a horrible book, because it tells of the wickedness of the Jews; that it records murders, wars, rapine, and evils of all kinds. We answer, the Jewish nation contained bad people as well as good. "There were vessels of honor and dishonor" in that great nation. God's writers in the sacred volume put the bad in as a warning and reproof to the race.

But the New Testament concerns us more than the Old.

If an infidel will admit that Christ was "a wise and good man," we can prove that the New Testament was written by inspiration, and thereby forever end the idea of no hell. Infidels say there is no hell because they deny the inspiration of the New Testament. We prove the inspiration of the New Testament thus: A wise and good man, in attempting the reformation of mankind, would prepare a correct record of his life and principles. Christ made no such record personally, because he *knew* his disciples who wrote the New Testament would be inspired to write it. "I will send you the comforter," he says, "who will lead you into all truth." "When you are taken before governors and rulers think not what ye shall say, for it shall be given you in that very same hour what ye shall say." "Lo, I am with you always, even unto the end."

We further analyze the New Testament thus :—

In order to the full exhibition of Christianity it was necessary there should be—(1.) A history of the life of Christ. This we have in the four gospels. (2.) A sketch of what followed His resurrection. This we have in the book of Acts. (3.) A systematic exposition of the theory of redemption founded on the death and resurrection of Christ. This we have in the epistles of Paul. (4.) A code of morality with injunctions and warnings against error. This we have in the whole New Testament. (5.) An exhibition of the mature results of Christian faith. This we have in the first epistle of John. (6.) A sketch of the futurity of Christ's kingdom. This we have in the book of Revelation. The New Testament is just what we might suppose it would be, on the assumption that Jesus of Nazareth was what he pretended to be, viz.: "God manifested in the flesh." The Bible, and especially the New Testament, is the visible link connecting God with man—this world with eternity. Shall we cut this link and thereby float off into eternity without chart or compass?

Dreams, visions, oracles, angelic visitations, conversations with God, inspirations of individuals, infusions of superhuman power, etc., are profusely scattered through the history of Judaism, and yet the glory of New Testament Christianity as far exceeds that of Judaism, in respect to all these and many other manifestations of God's power and presence, as sunlight exceeds starlight.

The indwelling of God was a mystery which was "hid from the ages and generations of Judaism," but this power was manifested to the Primitive Church.

THE INFIDEL'S END.

When the cold hand of death comes, you will curse the day of your birth, you will flee to the mountains and say, fall on me! fall on me! for I have crucified the Son of God. Henceforth there is nothing for me but eternal remorse. This remorse is the "worm" that burns forever and ever.

PAUL, THE APOSTLE.

Paul, The Apostle.

THE LIFE of a great man, in a great period of the world's history, is a subject to command the attention of every thoughtful mind. Alexander, on his Eastern expedition, spreading the civilization of Greece over the Asiatic and African shores of the Mediterranean: Julius Cæsar, contending against the Gauls, and subduing the barbarism of Western Europe to the order and discipline of Roman Government: Charlemagne, compressing the separating atoms of the feudal world, and reviving for a time the image of imperial unity: Columbus, sailing westward over the Atlantic to discover a new world which might receive the arts and religion of the old: Napoleon on his rapid campaigns, shattering the ancient systems of European States and leaving a chasm between our present and the past. These, (says a historian,) are the colossal figures of history, which stamp their personal greatness on the centuries in which they lived.

But I tell you of a greater than they. I tell you of

Jesus Christ, and of Paul, His great apostle. Compared to Christ and Paul, the greatest men of the world sink into insignificance. They lived and thrived for a time, in power, in wealth, in luxury, and then they went down.

When all things were ripe, Paul came. He came at the confluence of three national civilizations—the Roman, the Greek and the Jewish. The Romans represented temporal power and pleasure. The Greeks sought wisdom; the Jews religion. Aside from the Jews, the whole world was given to idolatry. For two thousand years God had sent upon the Jewish nation the rain and sunshine of religious discipline. They were His chosen people. The Old Testament is the record of God's dealings with the Jews during these two thousand years.

ORIGIN OF CHRISTIANITY.

When the time came in the providence of God, for the long-promised and much-looked-for Messiah to appear in the flesh, Jesus of Nazareth was born of the Virgin Mary. In time this God-man grew to manhood. Then came John the Baptist, preaching in the wilderness of Judea: "Repent, for the Kingdom of God is at hand." Then Christ himself began to preach, "Repent, for the Kingdom of God is at hand." He moved up and down

Judea, " and spake as one having authority." Vast multitudes followed him. He cast out devils, healed the sick, restored the blind and diseased, told the multitude who He was, and what He came for; that God, the Father had sent Him to point the race the way to Eternal Life.

This wonderful creature had nowhere to lay His head. He had no money. He had no friends. He never traveled. He never wrote a book. He was hated, despised, and finally crucified as a vile imposter. Then back He went to the bosom of His Father. The natural eye of man has never seen Him since (except for a brief time when He appeared to His disciples after His resurrection). He gathered to Himself a few despised indi 1-uals who believed that He was " God manifested in the flesh." They were as poor as Himself. They had no money and no standing in society, and were mostly fishermen. He told them that after He was gone, something (He called it the Holy Spirit) would come upon them and fill them with power. By it they could cast out devils and do mightier works than He had done.

His disciples went about telling that the Jews had made a terrible mistake in crucifying this wonderful creature. That He was in truth the son of the living God. Many believed it, and trembled with great fear when they realized they had crucified the Lord of glory. There was some doubt about His resurrection. He said He should rise again "in three days." Some believed it; some did not; and there were great disputings about it. Some even in this age deny His resurrection. But most decent people believe it. "If Christ be not risen," says Paul, "then is our preaching vain." "Ye are yet in your sins." It is of the utmost importance to know if this wonderful creature was raised from the dead, as He said He would be and as most people believe He was. The salvation or damnation of individuals rests upon their belief of this point.

This wonderful creature spake as man never spake before (nor since). His ideas appalled His hearers. He claimed greater wisdom than Moses. The Jews could not stand His teachings. They never had heard anything like it, and it made them *mad*. "Art thou greater than our Father Abraham?" "What makest thou, thyself?" "Tell us, 'Who art thou?'"

PAUL CALLED.

The teachings of this wonderful creature were taken up by one Saul, a man of great intellect and learning. He was miraculously converted on his way to Damascus, whither he was going, "breathing out threatenings and slaughter against the disciples of the Lord." As he journeyed near Damascus, suddenly there shone about him a light from heaven, and he fell to the earth; as in a trance, and he heard a voice saying: "Saul, Saul, why persecutest thou me?" And he said, "Who art thou, Lord?" and the Lord said: "I am Jesus, whom thou persecutest; *it is* hard for thee to kick against the pricks." (Acts ix: 2-5.)

"What wilt thou have me to do?" said Paul. The Lord told him his mission, and from that moment, Saul (or Paul as we now call him,) was this wonderful creature's most devoted follower.

For thirty years, in perils, on the land and on the sea, in daily exposure to death, Paul's devotion to this wonderful creature, knew neither interruption nor decay. For thirty years, in prison and out of prison, he served him with amazing effect. At all times, and under all circumstances he was true to his Master. His devotion carried him upward and onward, toward an "Eternal weight of Glory."

I am here to show something of Paul's life and principles.

When God wants anything done, He sends a man to do it. He called Abraham and Moses, and all the leaders of the Old Testament dispensation. When the time came He sent His son "Christ Jesus," into this world of sin and misery. For two thousand years He had been preparing the world for his coming. For generations the Old Testament saints had been praying and watching for the Messiah. At last He came, in abject poverty, and "His own received Him not." They entirely mistook the Messiah's mission. They supposed He would relieve them from the Roman yoke, and give them temporal power and pleasure. But Christ came in poverty, to turn the *hearts* of His followers from earth to heaven.

PAUL'S PERCEPTION.

Paul perceived the spiritual nature of Christ's mission, death and resurrection, more than any of his followers. He was learned in the law. His intellect was keen and his spiritual perception, under Divine guidance, most wonderful. His new ideas maddened the Jews. They hated to have their theology upset. It bore the consecrated dust of twenty centuries. It came from their fathers, and they hated to have it set aside. Paul's ideas cut them to the quick, and they sought his life. Religious people hate innovators. They prefer the good old ways of their ancestors.

In the books of Acts we have vivid accounts of the doings of Paul and the apostles while they were trying to introduce Christianity. The Jews fought the innovators at every step. Frequently the apostles were before the ecclesiastical and civil authorities. Sometimes they were scourged, sometimes imprisoned; but out of it all, "the Lord delivered them." They kept on preaching. They taught that Jesus of Nazareth, whom the Jews had wickedly crucified, was the true Messiah. Some believed, and some did not. Often a division arose among the Jews as to the guilt or innocence of the apostles, and they escaped punishment on that account. Paul was a Roman citizen, and this fact saved him many scourgings.

HOW PAUL PREACHED.

Paul was their great preacher. He traveled "from house to house," from city to city, from province to province, warning every man, day and night, "with tears," to find the Savior. He taught publicly and privately. He worked at his trade during the day and preached the Gospel Sundays and at night. He was "all things to all men," working, laboring with his "own hands," that he might not owe any one. At other times, "he hungered, and thirsted, and was naked, and had no certain dwelling place." His name became the "off-scourings" of the whole world. Whatever his outward circumstances, he stood firm. He called all his troubles "light afflictions."

His eye was on the "Eternal weight of Glory." Under his preaching the Gospel took root. Believers appeared on all sides. Churches were founded in the cities and villages, and Christianity commenced its march toward the conquest of the world.

I desire to put myself in Paul's place, and take you with me through his varied life scenes. Let us go back eighteen centuries. Let us suppose we live in Judea. We find that the Roman government is the only temporal power. All things visible are under its control. Its emperors live in the magnificent city of Rome, in gorgeous palaces, surrounded by retinues of officials, who are their abject slaves. The Emperor has absolute control over the life and property of his subjects. His dominions cover nearly the entire earth. His subjects are Romans, Greeks and Jews. Outside of the Jews the entire world is given to Idolatry and Sensuality. Paul was Christ's apostle to the "Gentiles," *i. e.* to the Romans and Greeks. Peter and the other apostles looked after the Jews. Paul's special work was with Romans and Greeks. He was to carry the message of Eternal Life to them. The Romans sought temporal power and pleasure. The Greeks wisdom. Paul, as the preacher of Christianity, had to meet the position of both.

During the reign of Nero, Paul spent two years a

prisoner in Rome, and of this experience I shall speak shortly. I now tell you how he came to go to Rome.

In the Acts of the Apostles we have a touching account of Paul's charge to the Elders of Ephesus, as he goes bound in the spirit unto Jerusalem, not knowing the things that should there befall him, "save that the Holy Ghost witnesseth, that in every city, bonds and afflictions" awaited him. But none of these things moved him. He counted not his life dear unto him. His only anxiety was to finish his Master's work. .He told them they should "see his face no more," and that he had faithfully declared unto them "the full counsel of God." "And they all wept sore, and fell on Paul's face and kissed him, sorrowing most of all that they should see his face no more." (Acts xx: 38.)

PAUL IN JERUSALEM.

Although repeatedly warned not to go to Jerusalem, Paul went, and, while preaching in the temple, he was apprehended and came very near being mobbed by some Jews from Asia. They moved "all Jerusalem" against him, and only the police saved him from death. They bound him and prepared to scourge him, but desisted, upon finding he was a Roman citizen. He was brought before Felix and charged with being "a pestilent fellow, and a mover of sedition among all the Jews throughout the world, and a ringleader of the sect of the Nazarenes." (Acts xxiv: 5.) He denied the accusation, but admitted he "worshipped the God of his fathers" in a way the Jews called heresy. Felix remanded him, hoping to get money. Finally he appeared before Festus, the successor of Felix, and by him was sent to King Agrippa. Festus sent a letter to the King to the effect that Paul had declared that "one Jesus" was *alive*, whereas in fact he was dead. Then the King wished to see Paul himself, and he was brought before him. Upon a hearing Paul defended himself, and the King was disposed to let him go, but Paul, when before Festus, had appealed to the Emperor at Rome, and to him he was sent.

PAUL IN ROME.

He sailed for Rome under an escort of soldiery, was shipwrecked, but "the Lord stood by him," and all on board were saved. After a time he reached Rome. In Rome he was guarded by a soldier, and lived "two years in his own hired house," preaching the Gospel with "all confidence, no man forbidding him."

Some of Paul's best epistles were written while a prisoner at Rome. Wherever he happened to be, in prison or out of prison, when the spirit moved him he sent an epistle. He always commenced it by declaring his authority as an "Apostle of Jesus Christ, by the will of God, separated unto the Gospel." Sometimes he wrote it with his "own hand." Oftener he dictated it, and sent it by some "dearly beloved" worker "in the Lord." They were publicly read in the churches, often amid "many tears." They were addressed to believers "throughout all ages," and in all conditions of life. His great theme, " Christ crucified—the hope of glory. Dead to the world, alive to God in Christ Jesus." Paul preached the Gospel " in bonds." but the " Word of God" was not bound. It penetrated the confines of the Roman Empire. "Your faith," he says to the Romans, "is spoken of throughout the whole world." (Rom. i: 18.)

ROMAN EXTRAVAGANCE.

In the time of Nero, *i. e.* when Paul was a prisoner in Rome, the Palatine hill (says a historian), had become one vast congeries of imperial piles for the private residence of the emperors and the officials of the court, and for some public purposes. It included palaces, temples, libraries, baths and fountains, the gardens of Adonis, and an area for athletic games. All this pile of palaces was rich beyond all modern luxury, in marble, and gilding,. and frescoes, and bronzes, and mosaics, and statuary, and paintings. There, the luxury of life, the extravagance of expenditure in furniture and feasts, and wines: the employment of troops of players, mimics, musicians, athletes, gladiators, charioteers, and nameless ministers of nameless vices, were such, as Christian civilization, in its most splendid and vicious periods, has never known.

Luxury, lust and murder went mad, in the house of Cæsar, from the reign of Augustus to that of Vespasian, *i. e.* during the very period that Christ and His Apostles were trying to establish Christianity.

These emperors were monsters of iniquity. They committed the foulest social vices. They were often vindictive murderers, killing their own relations, without mercy or cause. Nearly all met a violent death. They were too wicked to die like decent men.

But even, in " Cæsar's household," (*i. e.* among his slaves,) some were called "to the faith of Christ." They loved to hear Paul tell of Jesus and the resurrection. They were servants and slaves, but they were precious to Paul. He knew they would go up and their masters down. "All the saints," he says to Philemon, "salute you. Chiefly they, of Cæsar's household."

"Not many mighty men," were called in Paul's church. The Gospel was for the poor and needy. The self-righteous Pharisees hated it. The rich and noble missed it, and so it has been in all ages. "I came," says the Master, "not to call the righteous, but sinners to repentance."

"They that are whole, need not a physician, but they that are sick."

Timothy, Paul's beloved Son in the Gospel, to whom he wrote two of his most touching and important epistles; also Luke, the writer of the Acts of the Apostles, and Mark, the Evangelist, were among Paul's constant friends while he was a prisoner, "in his own hired house" in Rome. These, and others like minded, surrounded and cheered him by their Christian fellowship and affection. Great indeed must have been the strength which Paul derived from these brethren. Sympathy is sweet in proportion to the bitterness of trials. And their sympathy must have been doubly sweet to Paul, bound as he was "in chains," and living amid a most "awfully polluted Paganism." He speaks of them as "beloved," as "dear," as "faithful," and that, "long after," their converts in Christ.

PAUL AND NERO.

Behold a picture. Look at Paul and the Saints in Rome worshipping the God of their fathers, and the new God, Jesus Christ, just revealed to them.

Then look at Nero and his gorgeous surroundings.

Nero represented Paganism in its "utmost power, splendor, and corruption." Paul represented Christianity in "its feebleness, poverty, and purity." Nero and Paul represent, each, in the highest degree, what the world and the gospel can do for man. "The one tormented by conscience in the midst of boundless luxury and power; the other, joyful on the verge of martyrdom." The one possessing all temporal good; the other, scarcely nothing. The one rich on earth, but poor in Heaven. The other poor here, but rich, for ever and ever, in the Eternal World. Think of the infamy on Nero's name all these ages, and then, think of the power of Paul's words in the Bible all these centuries. Consider that they have been read and wept over by millions and millions, of the best men and women who have lived "in this vale of tears." Had you rather be Paul or Nero? "Choose ye whom ye will serve." This world or Heaven. "The things that are seen, are temporal; but the things that are *not* seen, are eternal."

"The powers that be," said Paul in the midst of pagan Rome, "are ordained of God." A strange statement for an ambassador of Christ to make, and explained on the ground that Christ's kingdom is *not* of this world.

PAUL ON DOMESTIC RELATIONS.

"Wives, submit yourselves unto your husbands as unto the Lord; husbands, love your wives, as Christ loved the Church," he wrote, while a Roman prisoner, surrounded by a horrible debauchery and licentiousness.

The Romans had not always been so depraved as they were during the time of Paul and Nero. During the republic, and even in the age of Augustus, the utmost purity prevailed in the family relations. The maidens and matrons were pure and modest. Adultery was punished by death or exile. Even the Emperor's own kin were not exempt. Unfortunately this law did not apply to the Roman father or youth. It was only the sanctity of the maidens and matrons that was so sternly guarded. And this, not on the ground of morality, but that, the " Roman stock might be preserved unmixed and unweakened," to the end, that the "state might always have fit citizens to uphold and extend the glory of all-conquering Rome." Outside of Roman families great license prevailed. Philosophers counted licentiousness, within the limits of the law, to be unwise, rather than wicked. This was Roman civilization—a civilization which entirely excluded all Divine guidance in the affairs of men.

Paul taught that to break the marriage bond was the greatest of crimes. It was to violate a specific law of God. It was to fill society with pollution, violence and manifold evil. If his views prevailed, it would close every brothel in the land.

IS THERE A HELL?

Paul taught there was not only a hell, *i. e.* a place of eternal torment, but that most people were in great danger of getting into it. Both Christ and Paul gave no uncertain sound on this point.

" Woe unto you, Scribes, Pharisees, hypocrites," says Christ, " why flee ye from the wrath to come? When ye see Jerusalem destroyed, then, know that your judgment is at hand. See ye not all these things" (meaning the Temple at Jerusalem); " verily, not one stone shall be left upon another. Think that I am an imposter now, if you will, but when you see Jerusalem destroyed, then, know that I am, in truth, the Son of the living God. When you see Jerusalem compassed with armies, then shall ye see the Son of Man coming in the clouds of Heaven with power and great glory, to judge the nations of the earth. Then shall there be weeping, and howling, and desolation, such as was not since the beginning of the world."

Behold the fulfillment of this prophecy.

In A. D. 70, or 40 years after the Savior's ascension, Jerusalem was razed to the ground by Titus, a Roman general, and everything Christ said was literally fulfilled. It was witnessed by Josephus, a Jewish contemporary of Christ, and who is acknowledged to be a historian of indisputable veracity on all those transactions relating to the destruction of Jerusalem. Josephus records the fact of the destruction of Jerusalem as a matter of history of which he was an eye-witness; but he knew nothing of the Scriptures containing Christ's prophecy. He speaks contemptuously of Christ as "one Jesus, a country fellow, who went about crying with a loud voice: 'Woe, woe, to the city, to the people and to the temple.'" The whole land of Judea is represented at that time as a woman "in grievous travail." Christ, himself said, upon *His* contemporaries should come "all the righteous blood shed upon the earth." (Math. xxiii: 35, 36.) And it *did* come. Christ's contemporaries crucified God's only Son, and therefore, the Almighty cursed them by sending upon them "such tribulation" as never was and never shall be again. The slaughter of eleven hundred thousand Jews and the awful overthrow of Jerusalem was the outward sign of that Spiritual judgment in which the Almighty judged the nations of the earth. The preaching of Christ and Paul greatly hastened the preparation for their judgment.

As the Jews could not escape the "wrath of God," neither can the Gentiles. "We must all appear before the judgment seat of Christ and be rewarded according to the deeds done in the body." The reward of those who patiently continue in well-doing, "and seek for glory, and honor, and immortality," will be Eternal Life —an Eternity of bliss. But to those who obey not the truth, but obey unrighteousness: indignation and wrath. "Tribulation and anguish," says Paul, "cometh upon every soul of man that doeth evil." To the Jew first and also to the Gentile. But "glory, honor and peace to every soul that worketh good." To the Jew first and also to the Gentile. The Jews, as a nation, had their judgment at the destruction of Jerusalem, and the Gentiles will have theirs at the end of the world.

PAUL'S SECOND IMPRISONMENT.

Before closing I desire to speak briefly of Paul's second imprisonment in Rome and his martyrdom. It may interest you as much as any part of this lecture.

After being detained two years in Rome, Paul was released. It is supposed he was found "not guilty" of the charges preferred against him by the Jews, and upon which he was held. He preached the gospel after his release in the provinces for several years, but was finally apprehended, and sent to Rome the second time, where he was executed under Nero.

It was a terrible time for Paul and his followers, when Nero, mad with debauchery and cruelty, commenced a systematic persecution of the Christians. Rome had been burned, and the opinion prevailed that it had been set on fire by Nero's own orders. The infamy of that horrible transaction still adhered to him. In order if possible to remove this imputation he determined to transfer the guilt to the Christians. They were condemned without sufficient evidence, and put to death with "exquisite cruelty, and to their sufferings Nero offered mockery and derision." The details of this persecution are too horrible for recital, and I pass them by.

I desire to call attention to Paul's spiritual condition while waiting execution. It was during this incarceration that he wrote his second Epistle to Timothy, which is so full of faith and apt in expression. It proves the sublime power of the gospel. It is no less remarkable for what it contains than for what it omits. He tells Timothy, and the faithful "in Christ Jesus," throughout all time, and in all lands, to stand steadfast in the gospel and to meet him in Heaven. "I charge thee, therefore," he says to Timothy, "before God and the Lord Jesus Christ, who shall judge the quick and dead at His appearing; to preach the word, in season and out of season, reprove, rebuke, exhort, with long-suffering and doctrine; for the time will come when they will not endure sound doctrine, but turn unto fables. But watch thou in all things, endure afflictions, do the work of an evangelist, make full proof of thy ministry.

"For I am now ready to be offered, and the time of my departure is at hand.

"I have fought a good fight.

"I have finished my course.

"I have kept the faith.

"Henceforth there is laid up for me a crown of righteousness, which the Lord, the righteous judge, shall give me at *that* day; and not to me only, but unto all them, also, that love His appearing." (2 Tim. iv: 8.)

THE END.

Methinks I see the old Warrior in his dungeon in Rome, waiting and watching for his Master. Look at him! Bowed with age. Chained like a condemned felon. Forsaken by "all men." Under sentence of death, and yet he faltered not; for he knew his Master would shortly appear and take him to Glory. For thirty years he had proved himself a minister of God, "in much patience, in afflictions, in necessities, in distresses, in stripes, in imprisonments, in tumults, in labors, in watchings, in fastings; by pureness, by knowledge, by longsuffering, by kindness, by the Holy Ghost, by love unfeigned, by the word of truth, by the power of God, by the armor of righteousness, on the right hand and on the left; by honor and dishonor; by evil report and good report; as deceivers, and *yet* true; as unknown, and yet well known; as dying, and behold, we live; as chastened, and not killed; as sorrowful, yet always rejoicing; as poor, yet making many rich; as having nothing, yet possessing all things." (2 Cor. vi: 4–10.)

Yes, yes, thou Paul, waited only two years for thy "crown." Thou wert executed A. D. 68, and thy Master came at the destruction of Jerusalem, A. D. 70, and gavest thee thy "crown."

Christ's Second Coming

AT THE DESTRUCTION OF JERUSALEM, A.D. 70.

This Lecture is a Key to the Bible—study it and get some new and important ideas.

Christ's Second Coming.

For eighteen centuries, Christendom has expected the second coming of Christ. From father to son, from generation to generation, this idea has come down from the Primitive Church. During all these ages, Christ, has *not* appeared in response to this expectation, and we are here to show that the reason He has not appeared is because He came at the siege of Jerusalem, A. D. 70, "in the clouds of Heaven, with power and great glory," and judged "the quick and dead," the righteous and wicked of the Primitive Church and Jewish Nation. This, is the proposition we propose to establish by a careful review of the New Testament.

We present the idea that Christ came in judgment at the destruction of Jerusalem, as a discovery, and ask for it a prayerful reception. No one can understand the Bible without *this* view of the Second Coming, and herein is the great value of the discovery.

In examining this subject we wipe away the tradition, and mist, and unbelief of past ages, and stand on the words of Jesus Christ concerning His own coming, and the expectations of Paul, and the primitive Christians. We imagine ourselves with Christ and Paul in Judea. They were addressing common people and we take them at their words. We believe they said what they meant, and meant what they said.

CHRIST'S WORDS.

We have the first reference to Christ's coming in Matthew x: 23; therein He tells His disciples, "When they persecute you in this city, flee ye into another, for verily, I say unto you, ye shall not have gone over the cities of Israel till the Son of Man come;" in Matthew xvi: 28, "There be some standing here, which shall not taste of death *till* they see the Son of Man coming in His Kingdom;" in John xxi: 22, "If I will that he" (John) "tarry till I come, what is *that* to thee?" which is a clear intimation that John should live till Christ came; *i. e.* till the destruction of Jerusalem, A. D. 70; in Luke x: 12, "That it shall be more tolerable in *that* day," (meaning the day of His coming when He would judge them,) "than for that city;" in verse 35, "To keep their lights burning;" in Luke xii: 36, "To act like men that wait for their Lord; that when He cometh and knocketh they may open unto Him immediately;" in verse 40, "Be ye also ready, for the Son of Man cometh at an hour when ye think not;" in verse 56, addressing the people, "Ye hypocrites! Ye can discern the face of the sky and of the earth, but how is it that ye discern not *this* time" (thereby meaning, the time of *their* judgment at His coming, then close at hand); in Matthew xxvi : 29, He says He shall not drink again of the " fruit of the vine " till He drinks it with His disciples in His Father's Kingdom ; in Matthew xxiv : 34, "Verily I say unto you, *this* generation" (by the words "this generation" Christ always means His contemporaries) " shall not pass till all these things," (meaning the destruction of Jerusalem, which occurred A. D. 70, and the tribulation preceding it and His second coming,) " be fulfilled." " Heaven and Earth," Christ adds with terrible emphasis (verse 35) "shall pass away, but my words shall *not* pass away," and therefore, we conclude, He came at the destruction of Jerusalem, A. D. 70, " in the clouds of Heaven with power and great glory," *i. e.* within the generation of His contemporaries.

In the 14th, 15th, 16th, and 17th chapters of John (he alone records it) Christ discourses tenderly to His disciples, (not to the world,) as he is about to leave them and return to the bosom of the Father. Among other cheering things He tells them : " In my Father's House are many mansions. If it *were* not so, I would have told you. I go to prepare a place for you; and if I go and prepare a place for you I will come again, and receive you unto myself, that where I *am*, *there* ye may be also." (John xiv: 2-3.) "I will not leave you comfortless; I will come to you. Yet a little while and the world seeth me no more; but ye see me; because I live ye shall live also. At that day" (meaning the day of His coming), "Ye shall know that I *am* in my Father, and ye in me, and I in you." (John xiv: 18, 19, 20.) "Ye have heard how I said unto you, I go away and come *again* unto you." (John xiv: 28.)

The above words of Christ are the foundation of the hope which has existed in the Christian Church, since His ascension, that some time He would " come again " to earth; and we are here to show that He *did* come at the destruction of Jerusalem, A. D. 70. He came exactly as He said He would, and as the primitive Christians expected, and yet, for eighteen centuries Christendom has known it not. Further on we shall show why they have not known it.

THE LOCALITY OF CHRIST'S COMING.

The locality of Christ's coming was " in the clouds of Heaven," directly over Jerusalem; *i. e.* at the place of

His greatest earthly agony. At His first coming He was crucified at Jerusalem amid the scoffs of the world. At His second coming He stood over Jerusalem, in the clouds of Heaven with power and great glory, "judging the quick and dead."

THE TIME OF CHRIST'S COMING.

We ascertain the *time* of Christ's coming thus: "Immediately after the tribulation of those days,"—*i. e.* immediately after the destruction of Jerusalem and the tribulation preceding it, says Christ, (Matthew xxiv: 29, 30, 31,) "shall the sun be darkened, and the moon shall not give her light, and the stars shall fall from Heaven, and the powers of the heavens shall be shaken; and *then* shall appear the sign of the Son of Man in Heaven and *then* shall all the tribes of the earth mourn, and *they*— *i. e.* the tribes, (see Revelation i: 7,)—shall see the Son of Man coming in the clouds of Heaven with power and great glory. And He shall send His angels with a great sound of a trumpet and they shall gather together His elect from the four winds, from one end of the heaven to the other." Again, he says (Matthew xxiv: 33), "When ye shall see all these things," meaning the desolation of Jerusalem and the tribulation preceding it, "know that it," *i. e.* My coming "is near, even at the door." Again, he says, (Luke xxi: 20,) " When ye shall see Jerusalem compassed with armies, *then* know that the desolation thereof is nigh," *i. e.* that Jerusalem is about to be destroyed, and my words concerning it fulfilled, " and when these things (he continues in verse 28) begin to come to pass, then, look up and lift up your heads, for your redemption draweth nigh," *i. e.* that I am about to come and take you with me to glory, and, therefore, we conclude: (1), that the destruction of Jerusalem; (2), the coming of Christ; and (3), as the consequence of His coming the " redemption " of his disciples, to whom he was speaking, were simultaneous events.

JERUSALEM DESTROYED, A. D. 70.

In the 24th of Matthew, Christ predicts the occurrence of certain events before His coming, which we now examine, and thereby show that every prediction He made relating to His coming was fulfilled prior to the destruction of Jerusalem ; *i. e.* prior to His coming.

In Matthew xxiv: 2, Christ says, " See ye not all these things ? Verily, I say unto you there shall not be 'left standing here," (meaning the temple,) " one stone upon another that shall not be thrown down."

History records the destruction of Jerusalem and the temple thus: " In A. D. 66 " (American Encyclopedia, vol. 10, page 2,) " the Jews goaded to despair by the tyranny of the Romans, revolted, took possession of the city, and a Roman army commanded by Certius Gallus, Governor of Syria was routed in battle before its walls." Titus, son of the emperor, Vespasian, regained it in A. D. 70, after one of the most terrible battles on record. His troops, maddened by the resistance of the defenders, spared neither age nor sex. Thousands of Jews seeing all hope lost, threw themselves headlong from the towers and a horrible scene of carnage ensued. According to Josephus, over eleven hundred thousand Jews perished in the siege, and ninety-seven thousand were carried into captivity. Titus himself, was unable to control the rage of his troops, and with regret saw the temple, (which he had intended to preserve as a memorial of his own victory,) burned, and the entire city razed to the ground; and thus, Christ's prediction, made A. D. 33, or shortly before his crucifixion, was literally fulfilled. Everything he foretold concerning the temple, city, and the people of the Jews was fulfilled in the most astonishing manner. It was witnessed by Josephus, a Jewish contemporary of Christ, and who is acknowledged to be a historian of indisputable veracity on all those transactions concerning the destruction of Jerusalem. The wars and rumors of war, the Antichrists, the famines, the pestilences, the earthquakes, the "great tribulation," etc., spoken of by the evangelists as events preceding Christ's coming, *all* came to pass prior to the destruction of Jerusalem. Josephus records the occurrence of these great events as a matter of history of which he was an eye-witness; but he knew nothing of the Scripture containing Christ's prophecy. He speaks contemptuously of Christ, as "one Jesus, a country fellow, who went about crying with a loud voice, 'Woe, woe, to the city, to the people, and to the temple.'" The whole land of Judea is represented at that time, "as a woman in grievous travail." Christ Himself said upon *that* generation (meaning his contemporaries) should "come *all* the righteous blood shed upon earth." "Verily, I say unto you, all these things shall come upon this generation." (Matthew xxiii: 35, 36.) And it did come. Christ's contemporaries crucified God's only Son, and, therefore, the Almightly cursed them by sending upon them "such tribulation as was not since the beginning of the world, no, nor ever shall be." (Matthew xxiv: 21.) All this would immediately precede Christ's coming, and therefore we conclude He came immediately *after* these events, *i. e.* at the destruction of Jerusalem, A. D. 70.

THE GOSPEL PREACHED TO ALL NATIONS.

In Matthew xxiv: 14, Christ says, "The gospel must be preached to all the world (meaning as it existed in His day), for a witness unto all nations, and then shall the end come." (Not the end of the world, but of the Primitive Church and Jewish Nation. They were judged, both quick and dead, at Christ's coming.)

Paul records the universal publication of the gospel thus, Rom. i:8, "Your faith is spoken of throughout the whole world" (meaning the world as it existed in His day). Rom. x: 18. Your faith is spoken of "unto the ends of the world." Romans xvi: 26, "That he had made known the Gospel to all nations." Col. i: 23. That the Gospel was "preached to every creature under heaven," whereof he was a minister. I Thess. i: 8, "Your faith is spoken of in every place." II Thess. i: 3, "Your faith groweth exceedingly." II Tim. iv: 17. That he had preached the Gospel unto "all the Gentiles." And, therefore, on the words of Jesus Christ that the end should come immediately *after* the universal publication of the Gospel, we conclude the end did come, *i. e.* the end of the Primitive Church and Jewish Nation, which He judged at His second coming.

THE ADVENT OF ANTICHRIST.

The coming of Antichrist is predicted before Christ's coming in Matt. xxiv: 5, 11, 24; in II Thess. ii: 3; in II Tim. iii: 1-9, 13; in II Peter ii: 1, 2; in II Peter iii: 3, 4; in I John iv: 1; and Jude 18, 19. In I John ii: 18, 19, 22, and I John iv: 3, we are told that Antichrist has come, whereby " we know it is the last time," thereby meaning that John and his contemporaries knew they were on the verge of Christ's coming, because the appearance of Antichrist was the *sure* sign that Christ would speedily appear. John wrote about A. D. 69, or a year before the destruction of Jerusalem.

HOW CHRIST CAME.

"Behold He cometh with clouds," (Rev. i: 7,) "and every eye shall see Him, and they also which pierced Him, and all kindreds of the earth shall wail because of Him." Christ, at His first coming, was crucified at Jerusalem amid the scoffs of the world. At His second coming He stood over Jerusalem " in the clouds of Heaven " judging " the quick and dead," (see Tim. iv: 1, 2, 3,) and they, *i. e.* " the quick and dead," *did* see His coming " with power and great glory." " For as the lightning cometh out of the east" (says Christ, Matthew xxiv: 27), "and shineth over unto the west," *so* shall also the coming of the Son of Man be," *i. e.* it was an instantaneous event, "in the clouds of Heaven." He came "with His mighty angels" (see II Thess. i: 7, 8, 9, 10) like a thief at night, snatched the righteous part of the Primitive Church, and the righteous dead of past ages, and hurried with them into Glory. Perhaps the memory of His sufferings here below, haunted Him, and He tarried not! He came like a mighty rushing wind, destroyed Jerusalem, judged the wicked, took His own, and back He went to the bosom of the Father.

This was the first resurrection and first judgment corresponding to the Jewish and Gentile dispensations. The Jews, as a nation, had their judgment at the destruction of Jerusalem, and the Gentiles will have theirs at the end of the world.

PETER'S IDEA.

Peter's idea, (II Peter iii: 10, 11, 12,) that Christ's coming and the "burning up" of this physical universe are simultaneous events, (and that is the popular idea about Christ's coming,) we are obliged to reject in view of his record as uninspired. He alone had that idea. Christ and Paul and John taught it not. And yet, even Peter expected the coming of Christ within the lifetime of his contemporaries. In I Peter iv: 7, he says, "The end of all things is at hand," *i. e.* I expect the speedy coming of Christ; in II Peter i: 16, he speaks of the "coming of our Lord Jesus Christ;" in II Peter iii: 10, "the day of the Lord will come as a thief in the night;" in II Peter, iii: 12, "looking for and hastening unto the coming of the day of God."

We live eighteen hundred years after Peter, and this globe has not burned yet. And, therefore, we conclude his idea, that Christ's coming and the burning up of this earth are simultaneous events, savors of the things of man, and not of God. Peter was a bold, impulsive, unlearned man. In many things "he was to be blamed." Paul "withstood him to the face." Peter "rebuked" the Master. No other disciple had the impudence to do that. He, thrice, solemnly denied the Son of Man in the darkest hour of His life on earth! In Luke xxii: 31, 32, Christ says to Peter: "Behold, Satan hath desired to have you, but I have prayed for thee that thy faith fail not. When thou art converted, strengthen thy brethren." In Ephesians ii: 7, Paul says: "That in the ages to come He (*i. e.* God) might show the exceeding riches of His grace in His kindness toward us through Christ Jesus," which opposes Peter's idea that the "burning up" of the earth and Christ's coming (which he himself believed was at hand when on earth) are simultaneous events. We believe Peter's idea—that Christ's coming and the destruction of this physical universe are simultaneous events—has darkened the mind of Christendom these eighteen centuries, touching His coming, more than anything in the Bible. If Christ and Paul had had such an idea they would have stated it. For eighteen centuries Christendom has argued thus: In II Peter iii: 10, 11, 12, it is said Christ's coming and the "burning up" of the earth are simultaneous events. The earth has not burned yet; therefore, Christ has not yet come. Therefore, we expect Him, and Christendom for eighteen centuries has expected Him—in vain. He never has come, (save as herein stated,) and never will.

WHY GOD ALLOWED PETER'S IDEA TO GO INTO THE BIBLE.

God wanted to curse the Antichrist part of the Primitive Church on account of their unbelief concerning the coming of Christ then at hand, and therefore allowed Peter's idea to go into the Bible. See II Thess. ii: 11.

WHAT PAUL SAYS.

Paul's expectations concerning Christ's coming we gather thus: Rom. xiii: 11, "It is high time to awake out of sleep; for now is our salvation nearer than when we believed;" Rom. xiii: 12, "The night is far spent, the day is at hand;" I Cor. i: 7, "Waiting for the coming of our Lord Jesus Christ;" I Cor. i: 8, "That ye may be blameless in the day of our Lord Jesus Christ;" I Cor. iv: 5, "Judge nothing, before the time, until the Lord come;" I Cor. vii: 29, "The time is short" (*i. e.* I expect the speedy coming of Christ); I Cor. xiii: 12, "Now, we see through a glass, darkly; but then (referring to Christ's coming) face to face;" I Cor. xv: 51, "We shall not all sleep (meaning thereby that some of Paul's contemporaries would live till Christ came, *i. e.* until the destruction of Jerusalem A.D. 70); II Cor. i: 14, He speaks of their rejoicing in "the day of the Lord Jesus;" Phil. i: 6, "He 'which hath begun a good work in you will perform it until the day of Jesus Christ;" Phil. i: 10, They are to be "without offense till the day of Christ;" Phil. ii: 16, "That I may rejoice in the day of Christ;" Phil. iii: 20, "For our conversation is in heaven, from whence also we look for the Savior, the Lord Jesus Christ;" Phil. iv: 5, "The Lord is at hand;" Col. iii: 4, "When Christ, who is life, shall appear, then shall ye also appear with Him in glory;" I Thess. i: 10, He exhorts them to "wait for God's Son from Heaven;" I Thess. ii: 19, "Are not even ye in the presence of our Lord Jesus Christ at His coming?" I Thess. iii: 13, He speaks of their hearts being established " in holiness before God, even our Father, at the coming of our Lord Jesus Christ with all His saints;" I Thess. iv: 15, 16, 17, He says, " We which are alive and remain unto the coming of the Lord shall be caught up together with them (meaning the 'dead in Christ') in the clouds to meet the Lord in the air; and so shall we ever be with the Lord;" I Thess. v: 2, " The day of the Lord so cometh as a thief in the night;" I Thess. v: 4, " But ye brethren are not in darkness, that that day should overtake you as a thief;" I Thess. v: 6, " Therefore, let us watch and be sober;" I Thess. v: 23, " I pray God your whole spirit and soul and body be preserved blameless unto the coming of our Lord Jesus Christ;" II Thess. i: 7, 8, 9, He says that the " Lord Jesus shall be revealed from heaven, with His mighty angels, in flaming fire, taking vengeance on them that know not God and obey not the gospel of our Lord Jesus Christ, who shall punish them with everlasting destruction from the presence of the Lord and from the glory of his power;" II Thess. i: 10, he speaks of Christ's coming to be glorified in " His saints, and to be admired in all them that believe in that day ;" thereby meaning the day of Christ's coming, which occurred at the destruction of Jerusalem, A. D. 70, when He judged the Primitive Church and Jewish Nation. In II Thess. ii: 1, 2,

3, he exhorts them "not to be soon shaken in mind" on account of the speedy coming "of our Lord Jesus Christ," and says, "that that day," (meaning the day of His coming,) shall not come until the "man of sin be revealed." In verse 7 we are told that the mystery of iniquity (*i. e.* "the man of sin") "doth already work." In II John ii: 18, and iv: 3, we again have the fulfillment of Paul's prediction concerning the appearance of Antichrist before Christ's coming. II Thess. iii: 5, "The Lord direct your hearts into the love of God, and into the patient waiting for Christ." I Tim. vi: 14, "That thou keep this commandment without spot, unrebukable, until the appearing of our Lord Jesus Christ;" II Tim. i: 10, He speaks of the "appearing of our Savior Jesus Christ;" II Tim. i: 18, "The Lord grant unto him (Onesiphorus) that he may find mercy of the Lord in that day" (meaning the day of Christ's coming) "for he oft refreshed me, and was not ashamed of my chains." In II Tim. iv: 1, 2, 3, Paul says, "That Jesus Christ shall judge the quick and the dead at his appearing," and exhorts Timothy "to preach the word in season and out of season," for the "time would come when they would not endure sound doctrine, but after their own lusts follow deceitful teachers having itching ears;" that they should turn away their ears from the truth, and "be turned unto fables" (thereby meaning that Antichrist was abroad, which was a *sure* sign that Christ would speedily appear). II Tim. iv: 8, he speaks of a "crown of righteousness" which Christ would give him at His coming, and to them also "who love His appearing." Titus ii: 13, "Looking for that blessed hope, and the glorious appearing of the great God and our Savior Jesus Christ." Heb. x: 37, "For yet a little while, and He that shall come, *will come*, and will not tarry."

JAMES ON THE ADVENT.

James' expectations we gather thus: James v: 7, "Be patient, therefore, brethren, unto the coming of the Lord." James v: 8, "Be ye also patient; establish your hearts; for the coming of the Lord draweth nigh." James v: 9, "Behold, the judge standeth before the door."

VIEWS OF JOHN.

John wrote in the very last days of the Primitive Church, and we gather his expectations thus: I John ii: 18, "Little children (how tenderly he speaks), it is the last time (as Christ is about to appear and take us with Him to glory), and as ye have heard that Antichrist shall come, even now are there many Antichrists, whereby we know it is the last time." I John ii: 28, "And now little children, abide in Him, that when he shall appear we may have confidence, and not be ashamed before Him at His coming." I John iii: 2, " Beloved, now are we the Sons of God, and it doth not yet appear what we shall be ; but we know that when He shall appear we shall be like Him." I John iii: 19, " We are of the truth, and shall assure our hearts before Him."

JUDE'S EXPECTATIONS.

Jude's expectations we gather thus: Verses 14 and 15, " Behold, the Lord cometh with ten thousand of His saints to execute judgment upon all." Verse 21, " Keep yourselves in the love of God, looking for the mercy of our Lord Jesus Christ unto eternal life."

WHAT JOHN THE REVELATOR SAYS.

We now examine the book of Revelation concerning Christ's second coming. In Rev. i: 1, we are told the things therein mentioned must " shortly come to pass "; in verse 2, " The time is at hand ;" in verse 7, " Behold, He cometh with clouds, and every eye shall see Him, and they also which pierced Him, and all kindred of the earth shall wail because of Him." (See our remarks on " How He came ".) In verse 11, Jesus Christ says, " I am Alpha and Omega, the first and the last "; in verse

CHRIST'S SECOND COMING. 63

18, "I am He that liveth and was dead; and behold, I am alive forevermore, and have the keys of hell and of death"; in Rev. ii : 5, " Repent, or I will come unto thee quickly"; in verse 16, " Repent or I will come unto thee quickly"; in verse 25, "That which ye have already hold fast till I come"; in Rev. iii : 3, "Hold fast and repent," " If thou shall not watch, I will come on thee as a thief"; in verse 11, "Behold, I come quickly; hold fast what thou hast, that no man take thy crown"; in verse 20, " Behold, I stand at the door and knock"; in Rev. xi : 14, "The second woe is past, and behold, the third one cometh quickly"; in Rev. xiv : 7, "Fear God and give glory to Him for the hour of judgment is come"; " and worship Him that made Heaven and earth, and the sea, and the fountains of waters"; in verse 15, "Thrust in thy sickle and reap, for the time is come for thee to reap"; in Rev. xvi : 15, " Behold I come as a thief"; in Rev. xix : 7, "The marriage of the Lamb is come"; in Rev. xxii : 6, He speaks of things which "must shortly be done"; in verse 7, " Behold, I come quickly"; in verse 10, " The time is at hand"; in verse 12, "Behold, I come quickly to reward every man according as his work shall be"; in verse 13, "I am Alpha and Omega, the beginning and the end, the first and the last." The very last words Jesus Christ says in the Bible are, (Rev. xxii : 20)

"Surely I come quickly. Even so." Says John, "Come, Lord Jesus."

CLOSING REMARKS.

We have now examined every verse in the New Testament touching Christ's second coming. Can any rational mind doubt but Jesus Christ *said* He would "come again" within the lifetime of his contemporaries; that Paul and the leaders of the Primitive Church expected Him, and that, as a matter of fact, He did come at the destruction of Jerusalem, A. D. 70, "in the clouds of Heaven, with power and great glory," and judge the Primitive Church and Jewish Nation?

In the interest of a sound theology it is of the utmost importance to know the truth about Christ's second coming. It is useless for Christendom to hope and pray for His coming, because it is a fact already accomplished. They may as well look it square in the face and adapt their faith and conduct to the fact. It is believed these views are destined to revolutionize the theology of eighteen centuries. Christendom must have a *new* theology—a theology to fit the fact that Christ came A. D. 70.

The great practical effect of this doctrine will be to establish the faith of Christendom in the Bible. This doctrine throws a calcium light upon the New Testament. It illuminates its otherwise mysterious words, verses, and chapters. No one can understand the Bible without *this* view of the second coming. It is a living stream of water running through the New Testament. This doctrine is the missing link, uniting primitive Christianity with modern Christianity, and, it is believed, Holy Ghost power will come to the church by a belief in this doctrine. Thousands have rejected the Bible, to their eternal death, on account of its apparent inconsistency, not knowing the truth concerning Christ's second coming.

This doctrine *ends* the communion: " Do this," says Christ, "in remembrance of me, *till* I come." If we behold His coming eighteen centuries in the past, an ordinance commemorating Him as a conquering Hero would be appropriate.

A correct knowledge of Christ's second coming is almost as important as a knowledge of His first coming. At His first coming He was crucified at Jerusalem amid the scoffs of the world. At His second coming he was a conquering hero. He then judged the Jewish Nation and Primitive Church, and since then He has ruled the nations of the earth.

Judgment, says Paul, comes first to the Jews; then to the Gentiles. At Christ's second coming God judged the Jews as a nation. For two thousand years, *i. e.* since His covenant with Abraham, He sent upon them the rain and sunshine of religious discipline, and the harvest was reaped at Christ's second coming. For nearly two thousand years, *i. e.* since Christ's coming, A. D. 70, the Gentiles have been under His care, and we believe the Gentile harvest is now at hand. We believe we are living in " the dispensation of the fullness of times " (Eph. i: 10, Rom. xi: 25) ; that the second resurrection and final judgment are in the immediate future, which will end the Gentile harvest. At the final judgment Christ will judge the world from His throne in heaven, and He has no need to return to earth for any purpose. It is not necessary, or even desirable, that Christ should return to earth again. When He was here He was badly treated. Heaven is a thousand times better than this sin-cursed earth. We submit, that our friends of the Prophetic Conference are in the dark, and we offer them this book, as the only rational solution of this matter.

We epitomize the history of the race thus: Adam, Noah, Abraham, Christ's birth, Christ's death and resurrection, Christ's second coming, A. D. 70. Christ's second coming is the pivotal fact of history. Standing on it we gaze up and down the ages. We look back to Adam and forward to the present. We can not extend the limits of this lecture. Hereafter we shall review history, profane and sacred, standing on Christ's coming A. D. 70, as the greatest fact of history.

In conclusion, men like John the Baptist, Paul the apostle, Luther, Calvin, Knox, Wesley, have been the world's reformers. Every one of them was a reformer, because he was a theologian who believed, and preached, and fought for the pure doctrines of the Word of God.

CHRISTIANITY REVIEWED.

This Lecture reviews Christianity from the Destruction of Jerusalem to the Present Time.

CHRISTIANITY REVIEWED.

IN the preceding lecture we have shown that Christ came for the second time at the destruction of Jerusalem, A. D. 70; that He then judged the Primitive Church and the Jewish Nation, and that the preaching of Paul and the other Apostles was a preparation for their judgment at that second coming. We also showed that Jerusalem was destroyed, A. D. 70, by Titus, a Roman general, and that the " wars and rumors of wars," the Antichrists, the famines, the pestilences, the earthquakes, the great tribulations, the universal publication of the Gospel, etc., spoken of by the Evangelists as *events* preceding Christ's coming, *all* came to pass prior to His coming, *i.e.* prior to the destruction of Jerusalem.

In this lecture we shall review Christianity on the basis of Christ's second coming, at the destruction of Jerusalem A. D. 70.

Josephus, and other historians, make no mention of Christ's appearing at the destruction of Jerusalem, because it was an event "in the clouds of Heaven" directly over Jerusalem.

At the time Jerusalem was destroyed most of Christ's followers had gone within the vail. Over eleven hundred thousand Jews perished at the siege of Jerusalem, and the abduction of a few despised individuals at such a time of carnage, would attract no attention. Josephus and the historians were too busy recording what happened on earth, to record what happened " in the clouds of Heaven." Besides, how could Josephus *see* what was going on " in the clouds?" "The world seeth me no more," said Christ, with special reference to His second coming. His coming in judgment was an event in the Spiritual, and not in the Natural world. His appearing "in the clouds of Heaven," at the destruction of Jerusalem, and the slaughter of eleven hundred thousand Jews, was the outward sign of that Spiritual judgment, in which the Almighty judged the entire race, except those living on earth at the destruction of Jerusalem. All who had lived on the earth, and died, were judged at Christ's second coming, at the siege of Jerusalem, A. D. 70.

There were two classes in the Primitive Church—those that expected Christ's coming and those that did not. An individual's belief or disbelief in His coming decided his final destiny. He appeared at the siege of Jerusalem "with His mighty angels," to those who were looking for Him, and took them to Glory. To those who looked *not for* Him, He came not. *They* were left on earth, and *their* seed has represented Christianity all these ages. *They* were the unfaithful servants of whom Christ so often spake.

On nearly every page of the New Testament, we find the speedy coming of Christ "in the clouds of Heaven with power and great glory," held up by the Evangelists, and especially by the Apostle Paul, as an event which would give to the "saints" of the Primitive Church, and the righteous dead of past ages, a secure and glorious redemption. It was the consummation of their effort, the reward of their faith and devotion to the Master, and yet, for eighteen centuries, Christendom has known it not!

The very curse Paul says (II Thess. ii: 11) should come upon the church, has been upon it since Christ came, A. D. 70. "And for this curse," says Paul (thereby meaning the unbelief of the Antichrist part of the Primitive Church, concerning Christ's coming, then close at hand), "God shall send them" (meaning the Antichrist part of the Primitive Church, and which Christianity since has represented,) "strong delusion," that they should "believe a lie;" and Christendom, for eighteen centuries, has not known the truth touching Christ's second coming. The reason they have not known is, because it was the *Antichrist* part of the Primitive Church which Christ left on earth when He judged the race at the siege of Jerusalem. It is *this* apostate Christianity that has assumed to represent Christ all these ages. As they forsook the coming of the Lord, so has the church, commonly called Christian, done in all ages. The Christianity of Paul's church was wonderfully different in spirituality and Holy Ghost power from any church since his time. There has been no power in the church these eighteen centuries.

APOSTATE CHRISTIANITY.

As we read the history of this Apostate Christianity, we are appalled at the record. And herein we find an unanswerable confirmation of our doctrine of Christ's second coming. Our doctrine shows that Christ's second coming *occurred* at the siege of Jerusalem, A. D. 70; that he then took the " saints " of the Primitive Church, and the righteous dead of past ages, to Glory, *and left the unrighteous part of said church;* and that this fact accounts for the terrible record of Christianity during the "dark ages." At that time, Christ transferred *His* interest in the church which He founded, from earth to

Heaven, and He is in no way responsible for the doings of the apostate part of that church since. It is a terrible libel on Christ to make him in any way responsible for the iniquity of that Apostate Church during the " dark ages." It was this Apostate Church that Martin Luther and his associates sought to reform.

" THE DARK AGES."

We now propose to glance briefly through the record of this Apostate Church, to the end that we may show the wickedness of its pretensions.

From the siege of Jerusalem to Martin Luther, covers a period of fifteen long and weary centuries. During these " dark ages" the Almighty seems to have withdrawn all interest in human affairs. Nothing can equal the ignorance, superstition, and licentiousness of *that* time. In the so-called Christian Church and out of it, iniquity was rampant. Many volumes have been written portraying the horrors of this dark period of the world's history; but it is not our purpose now, to enter into the details of that polluted period. We desire only to present a general view of the world during the fifteen centuries preceding the coming of Martin Luther, to the end, we may appreciate the work he and his associates accomplished during the Reformation of the sixteenth century.

THE ORIGIN OF THE CATHOLIC CHURCH.

After a time the apostates whom Christ *left on earth* grew mighty, and assumed by His authority full power over the body, soul, and estate of their deluded victims. They propagated this fanaticism with so much success that vast multitudes adhered to them, and they were known as the Church of Rome. The ring-leader of this delusion was called a Pontiff. In time, he and his cardinals, bishops, and underlings, grew rich and all-powerful. They claimed to be the visible representatives of the "dear Lord" on earth, and to have the keys of heaven and hell, and to do all things by His authority. In the course of a few centuries, these scoundrels grew immensely rich and correspondingly sensual and corrupt. The worst thing about it was, that they should carry on their iniquity in the name of "the meek and lowly Jesus," who had not where to "lay His head" while He tarried here below.

MARTIN LUTHER.

About the commencement of the sixteenth century these lordly Pontiffs became so corrupt and oppressive that the people demanded a reform, and Mr. Martin Luther, a poor and obscure monk, offered his service.

It is almost impossible for us of the 19th century to realize the horrible superstition, fanaticism, and licentiousness, which oppressed the people at the commencement of the 16th century. When the time came in the providence of God, for Luther to strike these corrupt Pontiffs, he struck them with tremendous power. He even startled himself, but he dare not draw back. He stuck close to God, the Father, and He helped him through.

The powers and emoluments of the Pontiff at this time were almost incredible. He had his emissaries all over his dominions, gathering "lucre" into his treasury, that he and his co-scoundrels might live in gorgeous palaces, surrounded by luxury and lust. He claimed, and the people believed, he had Divine authority to grant *indulgence* to commit the most horrible crime, and to gratify the most lustful propensities. He sent one Tetzel into Saxony, the home of Luther, to sell these indulgences, and this brazen fellow aroused Luther's indignation and set him to thinking. This thinking was the beginning of a reformation which set all Germany in motion, and proved of incalculable value to the race.

It was a bold thing for Martin Luther to strike the Roman Pontiff. In doing it he pierced the tradition and wisdom of fifteen centuries. During all this time the Pontiffs had been growing rich and mighty, and it seemed like madness for a poor and obscure monk to oppose them. For three years Luther stood alone. "Not a soul," he says, "for three years extended the hand of fellowship." After that, his views began to prevail, and then, "every one," he says, "wanted to share in the triumph." Little by little, the best minds of Germany surrounded Luther, and thereafter success was established. Germany had long groaned under the spiritual despotism of the Roman Pontiff, and it was ripe for a reformation.

Luther was God's man for this reformation. His genius was truly great; his memory vast and tenacious; his patience incredible; his magnanimity invincible and unshaken by the vicissitudes of human affairs; and his learning most extensive for the age in which he lived.

From this reformation came the Evangelical, or Lutheran Church, so named, in honor of its founder, Martin Luther, who sought to restore to its native luster the Gospel of Christ, which had been for ages covered with the darkness of superstition. His followers were moved to call the new church *Lutheran*, in response to a natural sentiment of gratitude to him by whose ministry the clouds of superstition had been chiefly dispelled, and who had pointed out to them the "Son of God as the only proper object of trust to miserable mortals."

The rise of the Lutheran Church dates from that

remarkable period, when Pope Leo X. drove Luther and his friends from the bosom of the Roman hierarchy, by a solemn and violent sentence of excommunication. From that time it has gradually assumed the dignity of a lawful and complete church, totally independent of the laws and jurisdiction of the Roman Pontiffs.

The leading doctrine of the Lutheran Church was that the Scriptures are the "infallible rule of faith and practice."

It was the work of Luther and his associates to rescue the Bible from the Roman Pontiffs. The Bible was exceedingly scarce at that time, and the few copies extant were kept under lock and key by the Pontiffs. Luther translated the Bible into German. He also inundated Germany with pamphlets on Biblical subjects. His great doctrine was, "*Justification by faith in Christ.*" He set the people to studying the Word of God. The more they examined it, the less power the Pontiffs had over them. Little by little their power was gone; not only in Germany, but in England, Ireland, Spain, Italy and France; in fact, wherever their spiritual dominions extended.

Next to Luther, as a reformer, stood Philip Melancthon.

After Luther's death, which happened in 1546, at the

age of 63, Melancthon became head of the Lutheran Church. He was a man of different stamp from Luther. Not so vehement, but more learned. His genius and culture were extraordinary. He differed with Luther on some important points, but otherwise they were in full sympathy. He was of the opinion that many things in the Roman church might be tolerated, which Luther considered as absolutely insupportable. This diversity of views after Luther's death created internal dissensions in the church, and caused much trouble.

If our doctrine, to-wit: That Christ's second coming *occurred* at the siege of Jerusalem, A. D. 70, had been known to Luther and his associates, it would have saved them a vast deal of trouble, and many long and wearisome and useless controversies. So with all the great churchmen of the past. They all missed the truth which it has pleased God, the Father, to reveal through us. The church records are full of controversies, touching the Lord's Supper, the Communion, etc., all subjects relating to Christ's second coming.

Christ said, "Do this," to-wit, the Lord's Supper, "TILL I COME, in remembrance of me." This holds good *only* till He comes. The church all these ages has not known of His coming, at the siege of Jerusalem, A. D. 70, and consequently has been taught to expect Him, and to commemorate His coming by the sacrament of the " Lord's Supper." Whereas, in fact and in truth, He came at the destruction of Jerusalem A. D. 70, and therefore, the exhortation to "do this," (to-wit, the Lord's Supper,) "till I come," is wholly irrelevant.

Christ, at His first coming, was crucified at Jerusalem amid the scoffs of the world. At His second coming He was a conquering hero. He then stood over Jerusalem, in the "clouds of heaven," judging "the quick and dead." And, therefore, an ordinance commemorating Him as a CONQUERING hero is only appropriate.

PROTESTANT CHRISTIANITY.

Since the Reformation Christianity has been divided and sub-divided, and re-divided, into the thousand and one Isms that curse it to-day. Notwithstanding this, Christianity has done great good and we are profoundly thankful for what it has accomplished. Its ascent out of the pollution and superstition of the "dark ages," has been accomplished little by little, and by painful effort. The Christianity of to-day represents the faith, and tears, and conflicts, of the Fathers. From time to time they have appeared with new light propelling it onward and upward.

We now propose to interview some of these Fathers.

And first comes

JOHN CALVIN.

He had some new ideas. From him came Presbyterianism.

As we glance through the records of church history since the Reformation, we are astonished at the trouble and dissensions the fathers have had from not knowing the *truth* about Christ's second coming. It has caused them more trouble than anything else. The greatest and wisest men in the church for eighteen centuries have not understood Christ's saying: "If I will that he " (John) " tarry till I come, what is *that* to thee ? " This refers to Christ's coming within the life-time of his contemporaries, to-wit: at the destruction of Jerusalem, A. D. 70. The church fathers have given it all sorts of interpretations except the true one. Not even our keen friend, Mr. Calvin, saw it.

The Presbyterians of this age are so eminently respectable, that we shall trespass upon our time somewhat, to give a condensed view of the great work of their founder, John Calvin. Calvin was born in 1509, and was bred to the law. As a student his success was "most rapid and amazing." He acquired the knowledge of religion by a diligent perusal of the Scriptures, and early saw the necessity of " reforming the established system of doctrine and worship." His zeal exposed him to various perils; and his connection with the friends of the Reformation, who were frequently committed to the flames, placed him more than once in imminent danger; but out of it all he was delivered.

Calvin had some new ideas concerning the decrees of God, respecting the eternal condition of men, and they stirred the people immensely. He maintained that the everlasting condition of mankind in the future world, was determined from all eternity by the unchangeable order of the Deity, and that this absolute determination of His will and good pleasure, was the only source of happiness or misery to every individual. He propagated his opinion by his writings, and by public discussions, and by the " ministry of his disciples." In time, it was inserted in the national creeds, and " thus made a public article of faith."

Although in sympathy with Luther, and the work of reformation, Calvin had some ideas of his own; and he pushed out for himself. He now had a large following, and they were known as the Reformed Church. He settled at Geneva, in Switzerland, where he acquired the greatest reputation and authority. He surpassed all the divines of his age in laborious application, force of eloquence and extent of genius. He was the head of the

Reformed Church in Geneva, and also acquired great influence in the political administration of that republic. His views and projects were grand and extensive. He not only undertook to give strength and vigor to the rising church, by strict discipline, but proposed to render Geneva the mother of all Reformed Churches, as Wittenburg was of all the Lutheran Churches. He proposed to establish a theological seminary for the instruction of ministers, who were to propagate the Protestant cause, through the most distant nations. He proposed to render the government, discipline and doctrine of Geneva, the model to be followed by all the Reformed Churches in the world; and he in great part succeeded in the execution of this grand scheme. His fame and learning induced many persons of rank and fortune to settle at Geneva. Many others came out of curiosity, to hear the discourses which he delivered in public. Studious youths came from all parts to the Geneva University, and its fame extended everywhere. By this means Calvin propagated his doctrine all through Europe. In the midst of this activity he died, in the year 1564.

THE Y. M. C. ASSOCIATIONS.

In August 1878, there met in this very city of Geneva, in a hall dedicated to Calvin, the International Convention of Young Men's Christian Associations. They came from the Protestant Churches, of all lands, to confer as to the best methods of pushing the Master's work. I wonder what Calvin would have said, if he could have spoken to them, assembled as they were, in his old home at Geneva. Methinks he would have seen the travail of his soul and wept for joy.

In these latter days, these Christian Associations have done a vast work in rescuing souls from perdition. About forty years ago the first one was established in London, England, by Mr. George Williams, a retired merchant. (He was present and took an active part at the Geneva Conference.) Since then they have multiplied in all directions. At this moment there are two thousand of these associations in different parts of the world. May God bless them, and their workers.

THE WESLEYS.

We now speak briefly of John and Charles Wesley. They did a great work for the Master. The former by founding Methodism, which has a larger church membership than any of the Evangelical Churches. The latter by his sweet hymns.

About the year 1729, the degeneracy of the times was noticed with sensations of horror by John and Charles

Wesley, who were students at the University of Oxford, in England. These devout brothers passed a good deal of their time in religious conversation, in reflecting on the contents of the Bible, and in private prayer. Other students religiously disposed joined them; and this was the beginning of the Methodist Church, which now extends in nearly all lands. A few years later George Whitefield, "a young and eloquent orator," joined the Wesleys, and he did great service in propagating the new faith, which began to make extraordinary progress.

Pure, Evangelical religion, as understood by Mr. John Wesley, was at length preached by him "in the open air and in the fields." He was compelled to preach "in the open air," as the established churches refused to give him a hearing. They supposed Wesley was propagating an error, and they sought to suppress him; but he preached on, and little by little, he had a church of his own. Modern Methodism is the result of *his* preaching; so it is in all similar cases. The world moves slowly, step by step. First individuals are raised, then groups, then nations. The public hate innovations—especially in religion. They prefer the good old ways of their fathers and mothers.

Mr. Wesley met with great opposition, but he continued to propagate his views with zeal and success. He sometimes preached "four times in one day," and in places quite distant from each other. Not content with preaching, he propagated his opinions by his writings. After a laborious life he died at the age of eighty-eight.

MESSRS. MOODY AND SANKEY.

We now desire to allude to the work of Messrs. Moody and Sankey, as it has been so marked both at home and abroad.

In 1872, Mr. Moody went to Europe, preached ninety times, produced no startling effect, and returned to America somewhat under a cloud. In 1873 he determined to try it again, and took Mr. Sankey with him; Moody was to preach, Sankey to sing. This time they met with extraordinary success.

In 1873, Mr. Moody felt impelled to go abroad, "to get ten thousand souls for the Master," but he had no means, and he would not ask man for the money to go with; so he prayed about it. He asked God, the Father, to help him, and He *did* help him. After making his preparations to go, with his wife and family, and Sankey's wife and family, and after bidding his friends "Goodby," at the very last moment help came. His steadfast friend, Mr. John V. Farwell, that eminent Christian and philanthropist, of Chicago, placed $500 and tickets for his company in Mr. Moody's hand.

After Mr. Moody had determined to go, an intimate friend said to him, "Moody, where are you going to get the money?" I don't know," said Mr. Moody, "but I believe the Lord will furnish it." After trying his faith the Lord *did* furnish it, and off he went.

MOODY IN ENGLAND.

After arriving in England Mr. Moody found that both the gentlemen who had invited him there, had just died. This was certainly a very strange providence, and it would have disheartened most men; but not so with Mr. Moody. "Every man," he said, "must make his own way," and he pushed out on his own account. It was in the rural districts of England, and in midsummer, and no one cared to be preached to. The attendance at first was small. Everybody seemed to be spiritually *dead*. It was desperately trying for Moody, but he kept on preaching, and little by little the people flocked to hear him. God stood by him, and great multitudes came to hear the Gospel preached and sung. Their march through England, Ireland and Scotland was an ovation. Their meetings in all the large cities were crowned with immense success, and no doubt many souls were saved for the

Master. After preaching two years in Europe, Mr. Moody returned to America. His meetings here have been equally successful. Wherever he goes the Lord seems to go with him.

We knew Moody ten years ago, when he was the laughing stock of Chicago. His zeal was so great for the Master, that he used to go up to strangers and say: " Do you love the Lord?" "Are you for Jesus?" Most people do not like to have their personality intruded upon in this way, and "Brother Moody" was considered by many people a nuisance. But these weaknesses are forgotten now. We see the work he has done, and thank God for Moody. Mr. Moody's knowledge of the Bible is wonderful; his delivery sparkling; his capacity to tell a touching story immense; and herein we see the outward cause of his success as an evangelist. But the real cause is, that the Lord seems to have a work for him to do. "Every man to his work," is the law in Christ's kingdom, and Mr. Moody is doing his work in preparing the world for their judgment, which we believe is not far distant. If the Bible is true, our belief that we are rapidly approaching the Final Judgment is true. There was a judgment at the destruction of Jerusalem, and there will be a judgment at the end of the world.

HADES.

HADES.

When Christ appeared at the destruction of Jerusalem, A. D. 70, not only Abraham and his seed, but the entire human race, (except those *then* living,) appeared before Him, and were " rewarded according to the deeds done in the body ; " *i. e.* they were judged; *i. e.* the " sheep " were separated from the " goats ; " *i. e.* the righteous went to heaven and the wicked to eternal punishment.

During these two thousand years, not only Abraham and his seed, but the entire human race (*i. e.* the dead part of it) were in Hades, awaiting their resurrection and judgment, which took place when Christ appeared at the the destruction of Jerusalem.

WHAT KIND OF A PLACE IS HADES?

We answer, Hades is the resting-place of the dead. It is neither heaven nor hell. It is the place where the dead (both righteous and wicked) await their final disposition. The righteous being detained for heaven and the wicked for eternal punishment.

The Bible characterizes the inhabitants of Hades as in a state of *sleep* (Dan. xii: 2; I Cor. xv: 51). But they are not in a state of absolute unconsciousness. They are simply withdrawn from the world of sense, like a person in ordinary slumber. They are in the *soul* of the universe instead of the *body*. Their operation on the surface ceases at death. Their sleep is opposed to the visible activity of this world, and also to the perfect activity of the resurrection world. After Christ's crucifixion He remained in Hades three days, and then He ascended to the Father. Before He ascended, He appeared to His disciples and said, "All power is given to me, in heaven and on earth," *i. e.* He entered upon a career of activity in both worlds. The saints in Hades sleep until their resurrection, when they, too, will be active in both worlds. The "saints" are said to "sleep in the dust of the earth," because *their* abode is not in heaven, but in Hades; *i. e.* until their resurrection.

Hades and mortality (*i. e.* this world) may be compared to two apartments on the same floor of a house. Heaven, or God's home, is the floor above. The resurrection is a transit to God's home. It is not a transit from one apartment to another. Enoch and Elijah passed

HADES. 95

into Hades by translation. And Lazarus returned from Hades at the call of Christ. Christ ascended out of Hades at the call of God. This same mighty power will at last draw "all men to Christ," (John xii: 32,) the righteous as well as the wicked. The dead, small and great, must stand before God. The paradise of Hades is not the final abode of the righteous. They are to be brought up for judgment and then pass into the kingdom of the Father. Hades is not the final abode of the wicked. They, too, must appear before the judgment-seat of Christ, and then pass into the lake of fire, which burns forever and ever.

As the Jewish Nation and Primitive Church were detained in Hades until Christ came and judged them, A. D. 70, so the inhabitants of this earth since A. D. 70 have been detained in Hades, awaiting their resurrection and judgment.

No person who has lived in this world since A. D. 70 can go to Heaven or hell, until the final judgment takes place, and therefore, if a person loves Christ he will be anxious to have the judgment come at once.

Paul (he was executed A. D. 68) only waited two years after his death to see Christ, *i. e.* till Christ came A. D. 70. Abraham, however, was compelled to wait two thousand years. It is fortunate for us who love

Christ that we live so near the judgment, as we are sure to see Him soon.

THE FINAL JUDGMENT.

Judgment, says Paul, comes first to the Jews, then to the Gentiles. For nearly two thousand years—*i. e.* since Christ judged the Jews at the destruction of Jerusalem—the Gentiles have been under God's care, and the Gentile judgment must be near at hand.

The judgment of the Gentiles and the destruction of this physical universe will be simultaneous events.

Once God said, "Let the earth be created," and it was created. Some day, in His own good time, He will say, "Let the earth be destroyed," and it will be destroyed.

Our idea is that the world is rapidly ripening for the final end. The war in Europe, now assuming large proportions; the extraordinary financial depression, at home and abroad, of the last five years, and the wonderful interest in the preaching of Moody and Sankey, all indicate that the Lord is moving in the affairs of men.

Just prior to the destruction of Jerusalem, Antichrist was exceedingly active. Men were preaching all over Judea that Jesus of Nazareth was not the true Christ, and professed Christians were falling away on all sides.

"They went out from us," says the apostle John, "but they were not *all* of us."

At no time since the destruction of Jerusalem has the spirit of Antichrist been so rampant as at this *very* hour. "We are coming to a period of great mental questioning, touching our religious doctrines," says an eminent Boston divine. "This controversy respecting future punishment," says a New York minister, "is an effort of Satan to unsettle the beliefs of mankind."

When will this earth end?

We answer, when the gospel has been preached to all men.

The exploits of Livingstone and Stanley show that the light of this century is beginning to shine even in benighted Africa, and the time must be near, with the electric flash encircling the globe, when it can be said, that the gospel *has* been preached to all men. Then, according to Christ, the end will come.

This earth had a beginning, and it will have an ending. To individuals, it ends at death. To you and to me, my friends, it matters little when it ends, if we have Christ; without Him we must perish.

Now that God is drawing near to earth once more, we need the faith, and simplicity, and Holy Ghost power of Apostolic times.

We believe these views are destined to unite all, who really *love* the Savior, in Tabernacle-form of worship, doing away with gorgeous and half-paid-for churches, to the end, that the glory of God in these latter days may cover the earth as the waters cover the sea. Let us labor and pray for this grand consummation.